Discovering
the World

Acknowledgements

Author: Neil Grant

Adviser: Ann Savours

Editors: Jo Jones
Trisha Pike

Art Editor: John Curnoe

Picture Researchers: Julia Calloway,
Anne-Marie
Erhlich

Illustrators: John Berry/John Martin &
Artists 4-5, 19; Eugene Fleury maps 8-
9, 12, 15, 16, 18, 20, 24; John Green/
John Martin & Artists 20.

Published by EMC Publishing
300 York Avenue,
St. Paul, Minnesota 55101

©Marshall Cavendish Ltd. 1981
Much of this material has appeared in the book
The Discoverers

This edition published 1983

ISBN 0-8219-0011-0

Printed and bound by
L.E.G.O., Vicenza, Italy

Discovering the World

The world that seems so small and easily crossed today was a frightening and unexplored place at the end of the fifteenth century. In little more than 300 years, from Columbus to Cook, the oceans and the continents were mapped to their present extent. This book tells how the ships, instruments and above all the explorers of the Age of Discovery opened up the four corners of our earth.

Contents

EMC Publishing

St. Paul, Minnesota

The Eve of Adventure

Six hundred years ago all travel was difficult and dangerous. Most people in Europe lived in the same place all their lives. A journey to the next town was something to talk about, and only churchmen, merchants, diplomats and soldiers traveled to foreign countries. Travel for pleasure belonged to the future; no one went anywhere unless he had to.

A journey by land, on foot or on horseback, along deserted tracks that disappeared in muddy marshes or tangled forests, was hard enough. A sea voyage was worse. Ships hugged the coastline nervously, fearful of storms and shipwreck. People who had to cross the English Channel or the calmer Mediterranean prayed earnestly for their safety and gave thanks to God when they reached the other side.

Some people had made long journeys in the past. For instance, in the tenth century, the Vikings had crossed the North Atlantic, settling in Greenland and visiting North America. Later, the Crusaders had gone to fight in the Holy Land, and Italian merchants such as Marco Polo had visited China. But Marco Polo's story of his adventures in the Far East was treated as a fairy tale, and the voyages of the Vikings had been forgotten. The Atlantic Ocean, the "Green Sea of Darkness" as the Arabs called it, lay mysterious and unconquered. No one knew where it ended, or if it ended at all. It was a greater mystery to our ancestors than the stars and the planets in outer space are to us.

The little that was known of lands far distant from Europe was a mixture of fact and fancy. Knowledge was based on travelers' tales (some true, some false), on ancient legends, on fears of the unknown, and on hopes of finding a better place. According to the Bible, the Garden of Eden was to be found somewhere "in the East". Some map-makers, therefore, hopefully marked it on their maps. India was known to exist somewhere east of Europe, but the "India" that people imagined was more like a

Above: The *mappi-mundi* ("map of the world") in the Middle Ages, based on religious teaching, looked nothing like the real world. The Bible said that Jerusalem was the center of the world, and the map-makers took that statement literally. The earth was shown as a flat disk, made up of the three known continents, Europe, Asia and Africa, divided by the Mediterranean sea and the rivers Nile and Don. East (not north, as on modern maps) was at the top.

world invented by a science-fiction writer than a real country. Everyone agreed it was a land of fantastic riches, inhabited by extraordinary creatures. There were men with dogs' heads, men with one eye in the middle of their foreheads, headless men with their faces on their chests, and giant ants that stored gold in their nests. Strange monsters lived in the seas, too, and many a sailor swore that he had seen a long-haired mermaid frolicking in the waves.

Most of these extraordinary creatures were probably born in the works of writers whose travels took place in their own imaginations, not in any real country; but others had their origin in fact. The story of dog-headed men, for example, may have come from some ancient account of a certain type of baboon, which has a very dog-like head. And the enchanting mermaid of the sailors' stories was probably a flattering report of either a walrus in northern seas, or a sea-cow in warmer waters.

At least mermaids were harmless. The open sea held terrors. Some men believed that if a ship sailed far enough across the ocean to the west, she would reach the edge of the world and fall off into Hell. Some thought that if they journeyed too far south, toward the equator, they would be fried by the tropical sun. Others, with more reason, believed that the sun would turn them black, like the people who lived in tropical Africa.

There were dozens of such tales, but in the 15th century educated men no longer believed them. They knew that the Earth was round, and they knew that it contained three great continents: Europe, Asia and Africa. On the other hand, they believed a fourth continent, as large as Europe and Asia combined, existed in the southern hemisphere. They knew nothing of North or South America, or of the Pacific Ocean.

In spite of these huge mistakes, they had some idea of the world as it really is. It was time for the ships to sail, to find out the true shape of the oceans and the continents.

Above: These "men" appeared in an edition of Marco Polo's famous book of *Travels*, largely treated as a fairy tale.
When so little was known about the real world, it was easy to invent creatures which were supposed to live in mysterious and far-distant lands.

Top and left: There is even a dragon here as well as a dog-headed man. Angry whales were shown engulfing whole ships.

Shipbuilding

The first requirement for building ships was a forest. Ships were built entirely of wood, and used up a great deal of it. A large warship built in the early 16th century contained nearly 2,000 tons of timber, or about 2,000 oak trees. Smaller ships took less but, to obtain the wood for four or five, about 200 acres of forest would have to be cut down. The best available wood for ships is oak, but unfortunately this is slow-growing. Faster-growing trees are less good as their wood splits more easily. Even in a country like England, which had many forests, suitable timber was becoming scarce in the 16th century.

Ships were built close to the water and, if possible, close to the forest. The *shipwrights* (shipbuilders), carpenters and sawyers were sent to select trees to be cut down. Tall, straight-growing trees were especially valuable for masts, and were often marked months or years before they were needed. Blacksmiths set up their forges in the shipyard to make nails and bolts, and other workmen began to make cables and ropes of hemp. The ship's guns and anchors were ordered from the nearest iron foundry.

There was little written material on shipbuilding before the late 17th century. The shipwright, like other craftsmen, kept his skills a secret (another word for *craft* was *mystery*, or something that is secret or hidden). Shipbuilding was often a family business, each shipwright teaching the trade to his son.

In spite of the secrecy, some kind of plan of the ship was made, though it was not followed as exactly as a modern builder follows his *blueprint* (detailed plan). One difficulty was that the weight of the ship was never known until it was finished. Shipwrights often made a model of the ship first, and sometimes drew a plan, cutting the timbers to fit.

The backbone of the ship was the *keel*, which was laid on wooden blocks. The *stem* and *stern posts* were fastened at either end. The floor timbers were laid across the keel and the *keelson*, a kind of internal keel, bolted through

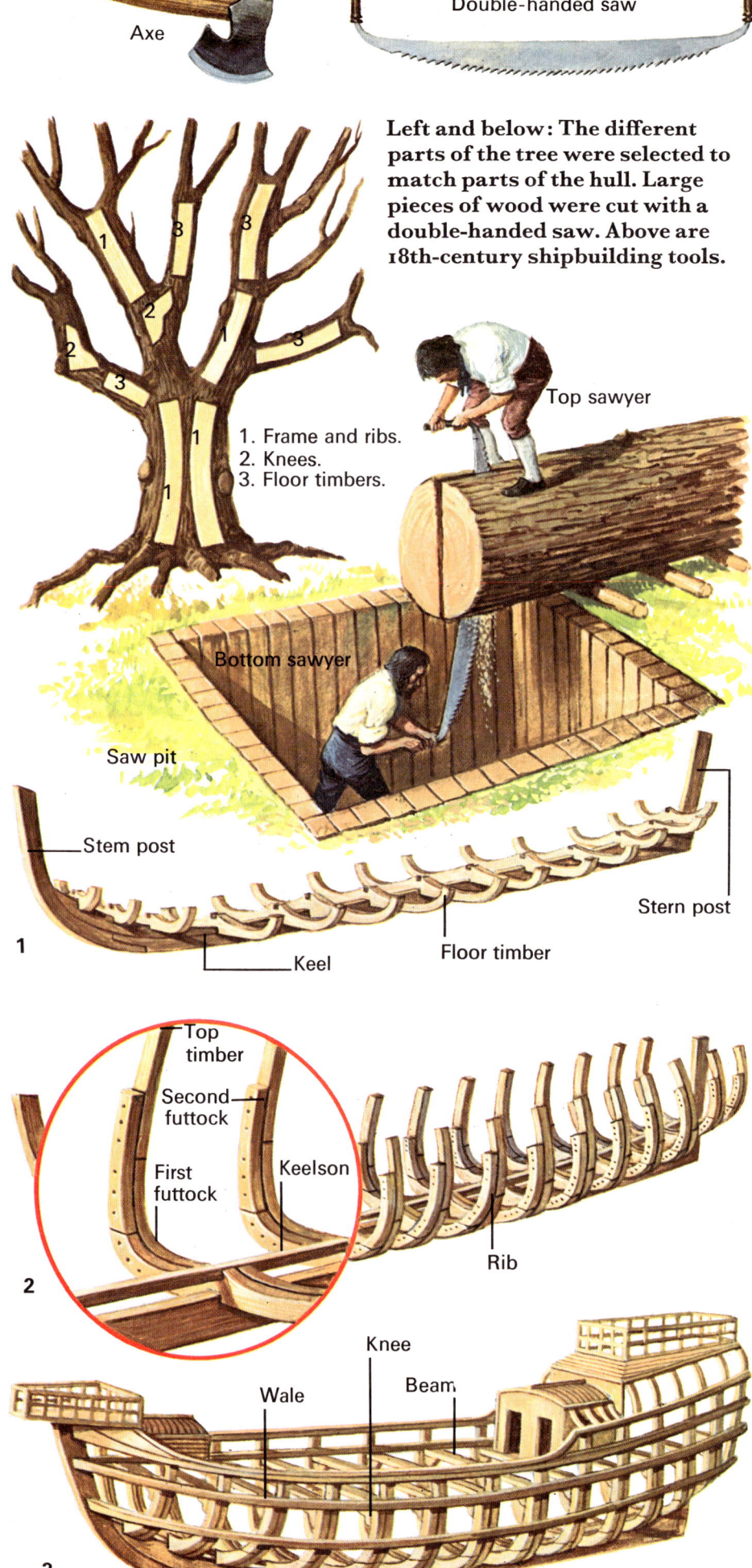

Axe

Double-handed saw

Left and below: The different parts of the tree were selected to match parts of the hull. Large pieces of wood were cut with a double-handed saw. Above are 18th-century shipbuilding tools.

1. Frame and ribs.
2. Knees.
3. Floor timbers.

Top sawyer

Bottom sawyer

Saw pit

Stem post

1

Keel

Floor timber

Stern post

Top timber

Second futtock

First futtock

Keelson

2

Rib

Knee

Wale

Beam

3

4

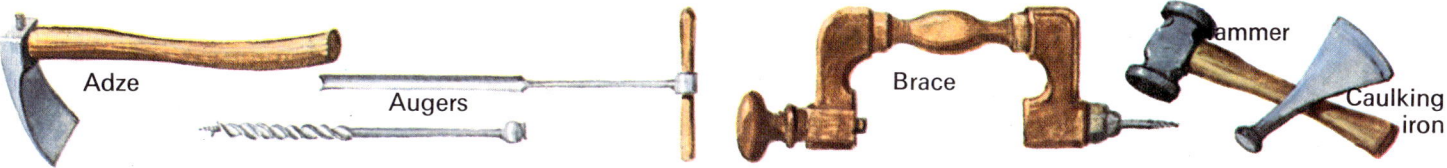

Adze Augers Brace Hammer Caulking iron

the top of the floor timbers to the keel with large iron or wooden bolts. The curved timbers forming the ribs of the hull came next. They were placed closer together near the middle of the hull, where the danger of breaking apart was greatest. Each frame was built so that adjoining pieces overlapped to make a strong joint. Shipwrights used to keep a look-out for naturally-curved pieces of timber which would be much stronger than wood cut across the grain to make the curved parts of the ship.

Scaffolding was raised around the growing hull for easier working and planks were fastened to the timbers, both inside and out. The planks, which had to be bent around to the stem and stern posts, could be up to 6 ins thick. The total thickness of the walls of the hull could be more than 20 ins. The planks were fixed to the outside of the hull with wooden pegs. These pegs were made secure with wedges of wood hammered in. *Oakum*—fibers from old ropes—was hammered into the seams between the planks to prevent leaks. The seams and the outside of the hull were then coated with hot pitch. This kept the hull watertight, though it did not prevent *sea worms* from eating into the timbers after weeks at sea.

The finished hull was launched, which meant very heavy work with winches and levers. It was then moored alongside a *hulk* (an old ship) used as a working platform or alongside a quay. From there all the masts and rigging were put in place. Before the sails were set, the hull had to be *ballasted* (made steady) with gravel to prevent it from rolling over. Once the sails were set, the ship would be very top-heavy.

Some ships were beautifully decorated, with carved wooden figures painted with gold leaf, and ornamental panels on the sides. The ships of the discoverers were plainer than the bigger and grander ships of the time. But they, too, carried very long decorative pennants and had painted sails.

Above: This engraving of the building of Noah's Ark shows early 16th-century shipbuilding methods. Tools being used include saw, hammer and adze, used for shaping timbers.

Left: Building the hull:
1. The keel was laid first, stem and stern posts fitted, and the floor timbers bolted to the keel; 2. The keelson was fitted above the keel on top of the floor timbers and the *ribs* added, built up with *futtocks* and *top*
***timbers*; 3. The ribs were then bound together with long pieces called *wales*, running from stem to stern. *Beams* were laid across, between the ribs, and secured to them by brackets or *knees*. Finally, the planks were fastened to the outside of the hull, the deck was laid and superstructures erected at bow and stern; 4. After the seams had been caulked, the hull was ready to be launched. The final stage, raising or "stepping" the masts, was done when the hull was afloat.**

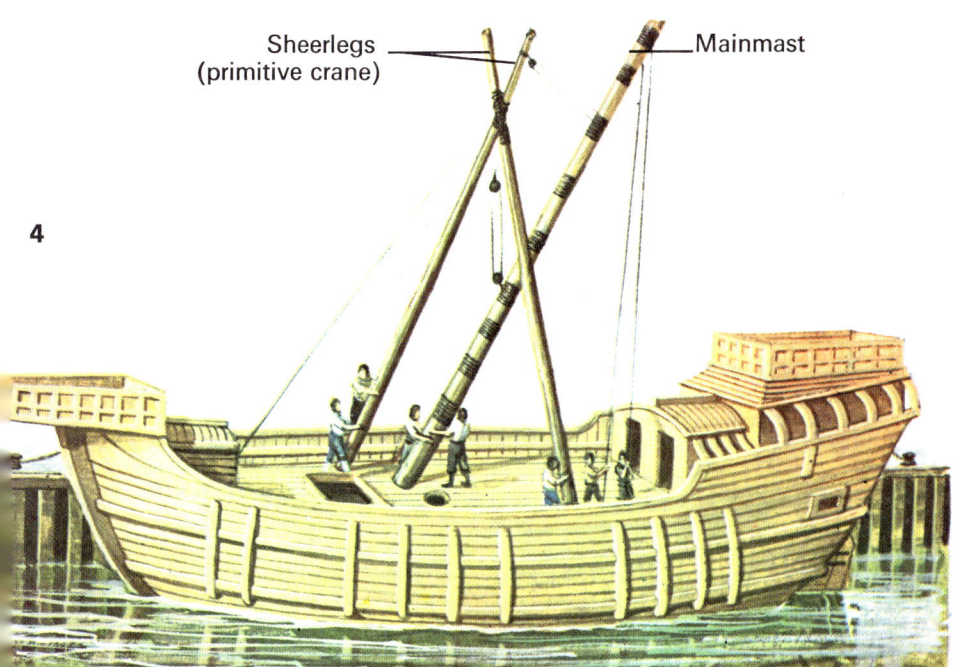

Sheerlegs (primitive crane)   Mainmast

4

Preparing for a Voyage

Discoverers did not set sail without some idea of where they were going. They did not always find what they expected, and sometimes the country they were seeking did not even exist. But they always had a destination in mind and a plan of how to get there. More often than not, of course, they had to change their plans before the voyage was over.

A captain could not sail off into the blue when he liked. He had to get the permission and support of the royal government of his country. Without these he had neither the money nor the influence to hire ships and crews. Some of the money might be invested by merchants hoping to make a profit from trade with newly-discovered lands, but most of the great voyages of discovery were made in the direct service of the government.

Ships were not chosen specially for their seaworthiness, or sailors for their experience in voyages of discovery. Someone who saw the ships being prepared for Ferdinand Magellan's voyage around the world thought they looked so old and battered they would hardly reach the harbor mouth, never mind the Pacific Ocean. In addition, some of the members of the expedition had never made a long sea voyage before.

Ships' crews were large, because many men were needed to handle sails, and because it was more than likely that some would die during the voyage. The captain was not always a seaman himself. He might be a soldier or a merchant, or a gentleman of the court with a taste for adventure. If so, navigation was the responsibility of the *first mate*, or *pilot*. The *boatswain* was in charge of the ship's gear, including the sails, rigging, and so on, and the *steward* was in charge of the stores. Below them, the most important members of the crew were craftsmen with special skills: sail-makers, carpenters and *coopers* (barrel-makers). *Caulkers* kept the ship watertight and looked after the pumps. Below them were ordinary seamen and one or two ship's boys, or *gromets*, usually aged about 14.

Some of the seamen might be rough fellows, quick to mutiny, but they were very skillful, practical men. They could convert a *lateen sail* into a square sail, or install a new rudder in the midst of a stormy sea. More than once, when a ship was wrecked on a distant coast, her crew managed to build a new vessel from the wreckage of the old, and sailed safely home.

One craftsman missing from the crew on early voyages of discovery was the ship's cook. The crew took it in

turns to cook, for not a great deal of cooking was done. Food was simple, because the provisions suitable for a long voyage in the 15th century were few. Meat was preserved by being pickled in salt water. For bread there was *ship's biscuit*—a flat loaf made from flour with as little water as possible, and baked very slowly until it was hard. It lasted a long time, though by the end of a long voyage it had become a pile of stale crumbs, heaving with black-headed weevils. Old sailors used to say that the weevils were more nourishing than the biscuit. Cheese and salted fish were often carried and with luck sailors might catch fresh fish over the side of the ship. Onions and dried beans were the main vegetables. The lack of fresh fruit or vegetables caused a disease called *scurvy*, which results from lack of vitamin C. Otherwise, the food on board was not much worse than the food most sailors ate at home.

Drink was a serious problem. Water does not keep for long in barrels and although ships carried wine as well, that turned sour after weeks at sea. Ships took on water at the latest possible moment. English ships sailing west refilled their barrels in Ireland. Spanish and Portuguese ships stopped at Madeira or the Canary Islands. Fresh water was the first thing to look for when a ship reached land.

These little, overcrowded ships had to find space somewhere for a variety of other objects that might be needed: lamps, tools, weapons (often including cannon), cloth and other trade goods, spare sails, spars, anchors, ropes, canvas, and so on. Some aristocratic captains took fine silverware, splendid clothes, and even musical instruments and a library of books.

1. Bowsprit; 2. Forecastle; 3. Anchor; 4. Foremast; 5. Movable capstan; 6. Ship's boat; 7. Sailmaker; 8. Main deck; 9. Chest; 10. Ballast; 11. Bulwark; 12. Hatch; 13. Mainmast; 14. Ladder; 15. Mizzen-mast; 16. Quarter-deck; 17. Cabin for officers of ship's company; 18. Captain's cabin; 19. Captain's bunk; 20. Poop; 21. Tiller; 22. Rudder; 23. Ship's stores included all materials for repairing ship, eg sailcloth, rope. Casks, jars, baskets, sacks held water, wine, oil, flour, bacon, vinegar, peas, beans, dried fish, rice, honey, cheese and raisins.

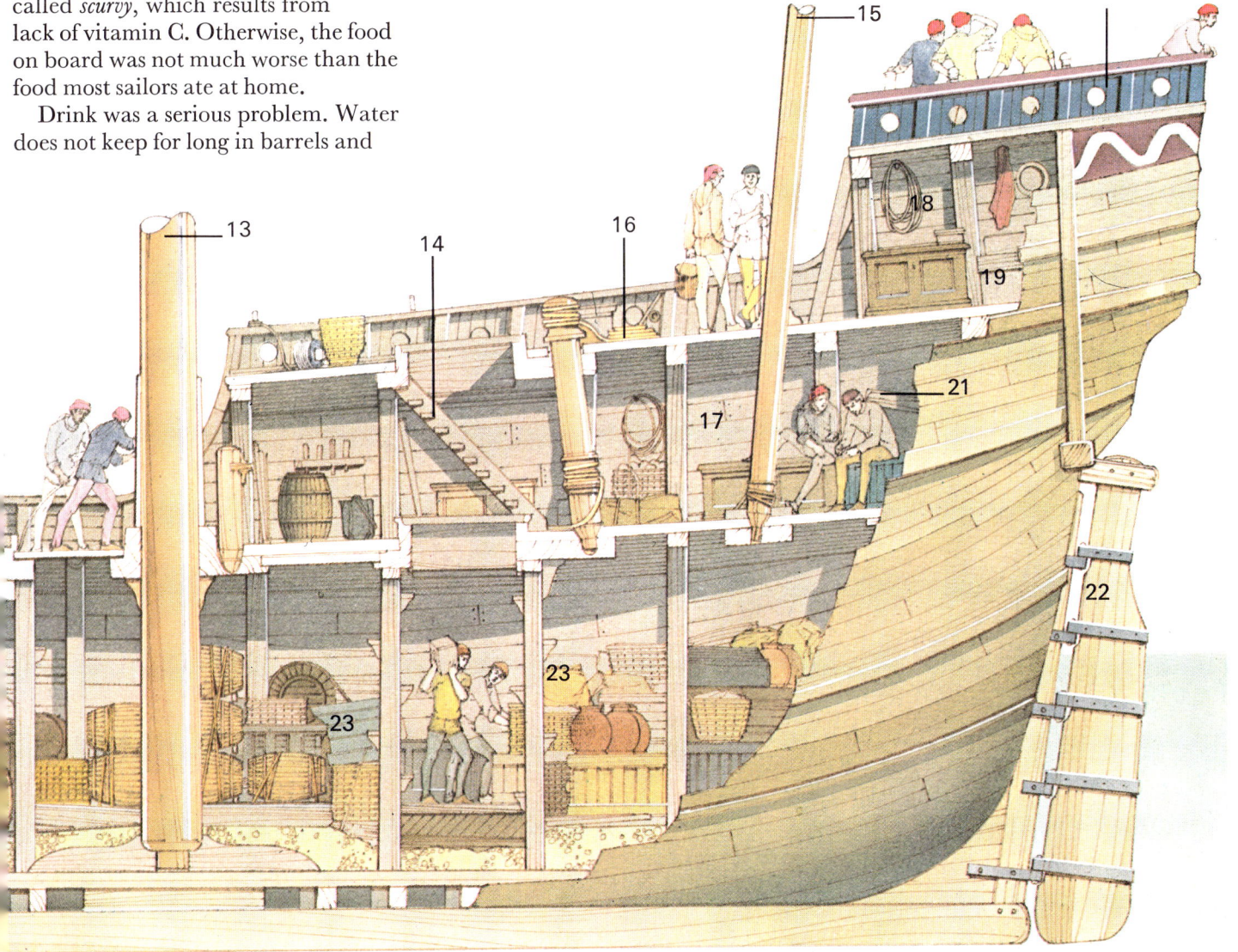

Columbus

While the Portuguese were creating their trade empire in the East, their Spanish neighbors were building an empire in the west, where a New World had been discovered. The man who discovered the New World for Spain was one of the most famous explorers, Christopher Columbus.

Columbus was an Italian, but he had settled in Portugal as a young man. It was there he became interested in the problem of trade routes to the Far East. The Portuguese were trying to reach Asia by sailing around Africa and across the Indian Ocean, but Columbus had a different idea. He believed that the easiest way to reach the East was by sailing west. As the Earth is round, a ship would sooner or later reach the Far East from the opposite direction; it was only necessary to look at a world globe to see that was possible. Columbus believed that the westward route would be the quickest.

But Columbus's globe did not give a true picture of the world. In the northern hemisphere it showed a single land mass, Europe and Asia, whose eastern and western coasts were separated by the Atlantic Ocean. The existence of the continents of North and South America was unknown and unsuspected. And no one knew there was a Pacific Ocean.

Columbus's map was incorrect in other ways. It made the Earth smaller than it really is by nearly one-third. It also made Asia stretch too far to the east. As a result, the voyage from Europe to Asia appeared fairly simple. Columbus calculated that the distance between the Canary Islands and Japan was 2,400 nautical miles. By coincidence, this is very close to the distance across the Atlantic.

Having decided that the voyage was possible, Columbus's next step was to gain government support. He laid his plan before the Portuguese government, but they turned it down. The Portuguese were not interested in a westward route because their captains were already exploring the route via the Indian Ocean. Columbus turned to other

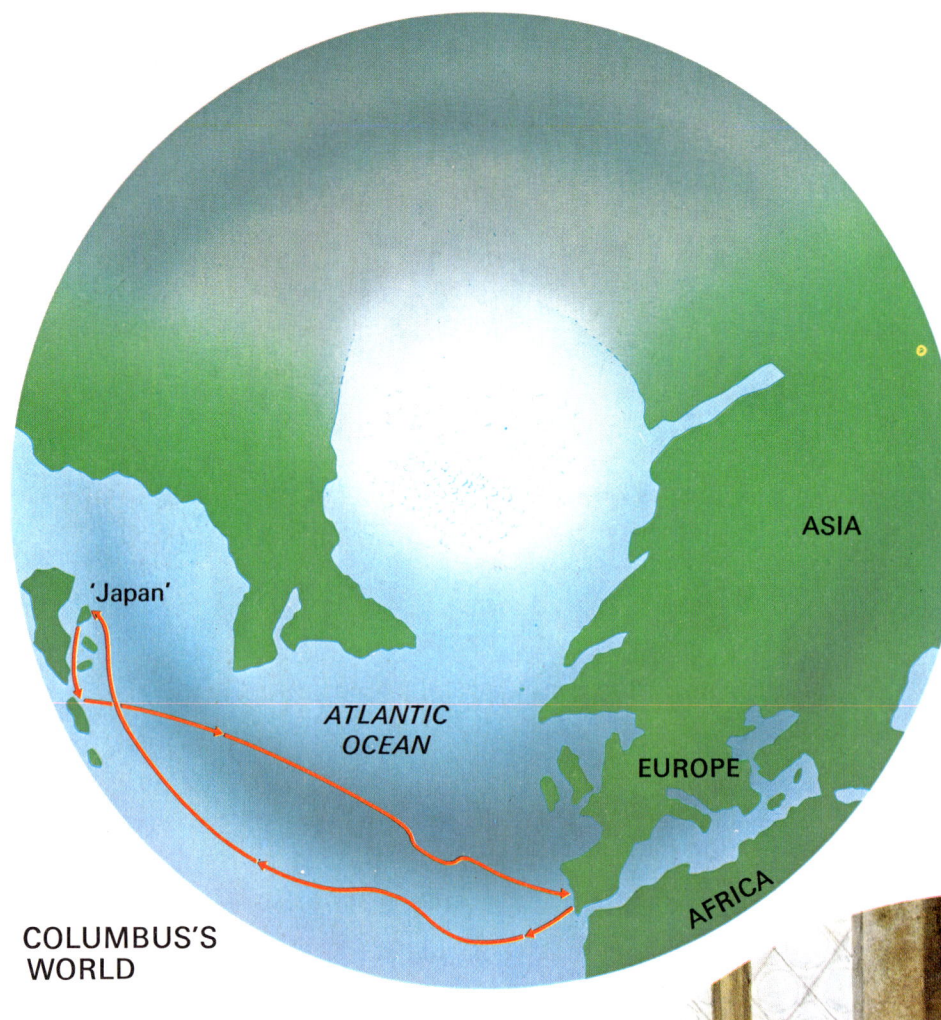

COLUMBUS'S WORLD

Above: These globes show Columbus's Atlantic voyage in 1492. The first one shows the world as Columbus thought it was, and the second the world as it really is.

Right: In 1491 Columbus explained his ideas to the Prior of the Abbey of La Rábida, where his son was at school. The Prior persuaded him to wait for Queen Isabella's help.

governments. His brother Bartholomew tried the kings of England and France, but without success. Meanwhile Christopher went to Spain. He had already been in touch with Queen Isabella, and a Spanish commission had been appointed to study his plan. After long delay, the commissioners reported that the plan was unsound. The ocean, they said, was much larger than Columbus believed, and the voyage would take far longer.

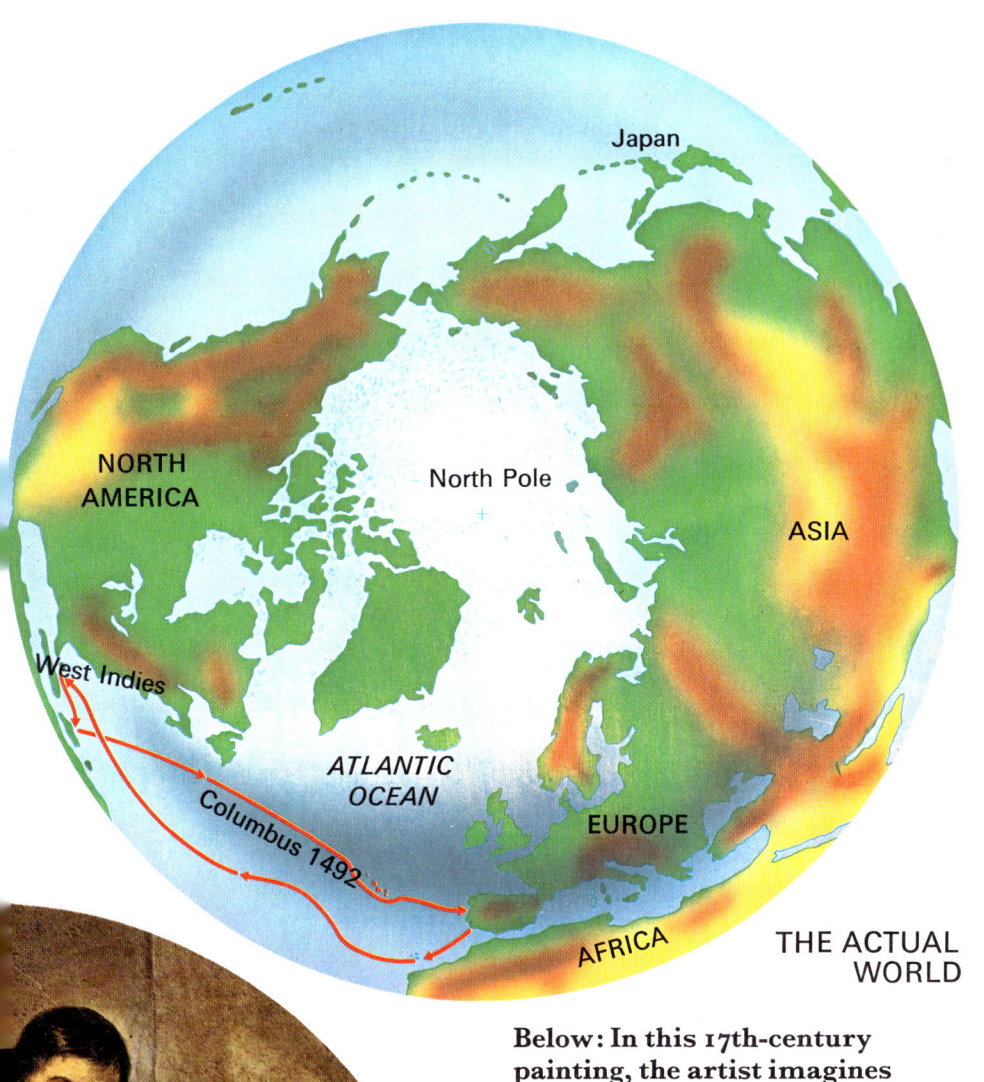

THE ACTUAL
WORLD

They were, of course, quite right!
Columbus could not agree with them
and the Queen sympathetically advised
him to wait a while and apply again.

But again the Spanish experts
reported unfavorably. Columbus
packed his bags, saddled his mule, and
prepared to leave the country. He had
gone several miles when a messenger
from Queen Isabella caught up with
him. The Queen had always liked
Columbus, and now she said she
would pawn the crown jewels, if
necessary, to raise enough money for
his expedition.

Preparations for the voyage took
just over three months. Columbus's
flagship was the *Santa Maria*. In the
custom of the time she carried a huge
square sail on her main mast and a
smaller one on the foremast. The
mizzen mast, on the high poop at the
stern, was lateen-rigged. He also had
two *caravels*, the *Niña*, lateen-rigged,
and the square-rigged *Pinta*.

On 3 August 1492 the three ships
set sail. In a little over a week, the
northerly winds brought them to the
Canary Islands, where Columbus had
the *Niña* converted to square rig,
since she was lagging behind the
others. The water casks were refilled
and fresh food bought. On 6
September, the ships weighed anchor
and set sail due west, heading for
unknown waters.

**Below: In this 17th-century
painting, the artist imagines
how Columbus presented to the
Spanish King Ferdinand and
Queen Isabella the evidence of his
discovery of what he thought was
the sea route to Asia.**

9

In Columbus's Ships

It is hard to imagine anything more adventurous than a voyage of discovery. Yet day-to-day life on board Columbus's ships, like life in a space satellite today, was often rather boring. The day was divided into watches, and each watch into half-hours measured by a *sand-glass*. As soon as the sand trickled down, marking the end of a half-hour, one of the ship's boys would turn it over. Time was checked every day at noon, when the sun lay due south according to the *compass*.

Columbus's ships made good speed, covering as much as 150 miles a day: a modern yacht does not go much faster. Yet Columbus slightly over-estimated his speed. The result was that he calculated his position at the end of his voyage a little farther west than it was. He sailed along a *line of latitude*—that is due east or due west—as navigators always did when possible, and with a following wind. This meant that the actual sailing of the ship, including manning the sails and navigating the course, was not particularly difficult.

A sailor's life is always hard, but a modern sailor would certainly have found Columbus's ships very uncomfortable. A sailor then could never be certain of getting a hot meal. Food was cooked in a box, bedded in sand as a precaution against fire, on the open deck. Although the fire was protected by a hood, it was impossible to do much cooking in stormy weather. The food was dull, as nearly everything was dried or salted, but enough—if the voyage was not too long.

There were no bathrooms on board, and no one took his boots off at night. The captain had a wooden bunk in his little cabin, but the crew slept where and how they could. In fine weather they would lie on the open deck, but if it was raining they had to find a corner among the cargo and ballast in the hold. In the West Indies, Columbus noticed the natives used hammocks slung between two trees. Soon afterwards, hammocks were introduced to European ships, and made life less uncomfortable.

In Columbus's day, religion had a powerful hold on people. Each exploring voyage was, among other things, a missionary expedition, since every man believed it was his duty to spread Christianity among non-Christian peoples. God was seldom forgotten even in the ordinary running of the ship. The day began with prayers and a hymn, sung by one of the ship's boys. The sea chanteys of the time were often religious songs; the boy who turned the sand-glass at the end of the watch would sing a little song like this:

The watch is called,
The glass floweth.
We shall make a good voyage
If God willeth.

There was a religious service in the evening, too, attended by every member of the crew. But, as Columbus himself said, a company of unmusical seamen bawling the words of a Latin chant which they did not understand was hard on the ears!

After a month at sea without sight of land, the crew became restless. Ominous mutterings were heard among those off duty. Then, as often happens when a crowd of strangers are cooped up together, tempers grew short, arguments broke out, and mutiny boiled up. The authority of Columbus himself was weak because he was a foreigner who spoke the language of his men with a strong accent. Fortunately, he was loyally supported by his Spanish captains. But on 9 October he was forced to promise that he would turn back if no land was sighted.

Two days later drifting leaves and branches appeared, a sure sign of land nearby. Soon after midnight the look-out on the *Pinta* yelled out, "Land!" Sandy cliffs appeared in the distance. When day came the ship found an anchorage, and Columbus stepped ashore on a white coral beach. He gave thanks to God, believing he had found an island of the East Indies. The truth was he had discovered the West Indies. The little island where he landed was one of the Bahamas, now known as Watlings Island.

Above: In the West Indies Columbus noticed the people slept in hammocks (top left) slung between trees. This idea was adopted in European ships.

Below: The "Indians" meet the Spaniards. Columbus called the people of the Americas "Indians" because he thought he was in the East Indies. Their peaceful nature made it easy for the Spaniards to make them slaves.

Above: The *Santa Maria* was the largest and most famous of Columbus's ships. This is what she may have looked like.
1. Ladder from quarterdeck to main deck; 2. Poop deck; 3. Hatch; 4. Spritsail; 5. Foresail; 6. Mainsail; 7. Topsail; 8. Lateen sail; 9. Top castle.

Right: Christopher Columbus.

Treasures of Montezuma

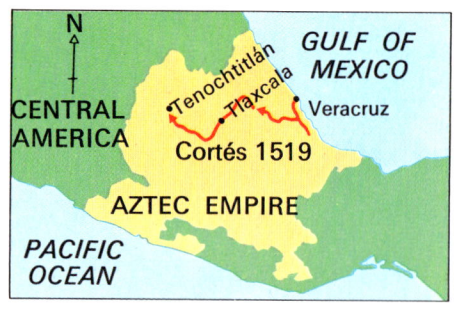

Above and left: The map shows the area controlled by the Aztecs in Mexico and the route taken by Cortés. The Aztecs ruled Central America by their skill in war. Although bloodshed was commonplace, they found enjoyment in music and flowers.

Right: The Aztec ruler carried by his people.

Like the Portuguese in their eastern exploration, the Spaniards discovered new societies in the west. But the people of North and South America were more foreign to Europeans than the people of Asia, and their technology was far less advanced. The Asians were surprised by the power of Portuguese ships and guns, but at least they knew what these things were. The people of the New World had never heard a gun fired, nor seen a sailing ship. They had no metal tools, no plows or carts (they had never invented the wheel), and they had never seen a horse. Some of them had developed wealthy, complicated

civilizations with great stone cities, rich in treasure. Their richness, combined with their weakness, proved fatal. They were ill-prepared to resist the armed and mounted Spaniards who, fierce as wolves in their desire for gold and glory, descended upon them in the years after Columbus's discovery.

The Spaniards first settled in the West Indies, cruelly killing and enslaving the natives in thousands. In 1519 the Spanish governor of Cuba sent an expedition, commanded by Hernán Cortés, to investigate rumors of a rich kingdom in Mexico. The purpose of the expedition was to

explore, and perhaps seize slaves and treasure. But the ambitious Cortés had bigger ideas. He hoped to gain a kingdom for himself.

Cortés landed at Veracruz and defeated the local people in battle. He learned from them that the rulers of the country were the Aztecs, whose capital was at Tenochtitlán, near the modern Mexico City. The Aztecs were not loved by the people they ruled, and the Spaniards found many allies willing to help them. Otherwise, five hundred ragged Spanish soldiers could never have conquered an empire of five million people.

From Veracruz the Spaniards advanced through steamy jungle, to the high central plain of Mexico. They made their base at Tlaxcala, a city independent of the Aztecs, though often raided by them. Messengers from Montezuma, the Aztec war leader, reached them there. The messages were threatening but Cortés, who was no fool, detected fear lurking behind the threats. Also the greed of his men was whetted by

Left: The Aztecs were skilled at covering objects in turquoise mosaics. This is a breastplate ornament in the form of a double-headed serpent.

the rich presents which the messengers bore. Cortés politely insisted on entering Tenochtitlán, and Montezuma agreed to admit him. It was surprising that the Aztec leader was so trusting, but he may have belived that Hernán Cortés was the Aztec god himself, Quetzalcoatl. According to legend, this god was due to return to earth one day.

The sight of Tenochtitlán satisfied the Spaniards' wildest dreams of treasure. The city was built on islands in a lake, reached by a narrow causeway. Dazzling stone towers climbed toward the sky, gardens rose in terraces from broad straight streets, and canoes paddled back and forth along canals. From the temple where human sacrifices were made to the gods, a flight of 114 steps led down to the ground.

The Spaniards entered the city peacefully, but while Cortés was away his crowd of unruly adventurers quarreled with their hosts, destroying the temples and seizing booty. When Cortés returned, he found his army trapped in a hostile city. Montezuma was stoned to death while trying to pacify his angry people. The Spaniards had to fight their way out along the causeway. Back in Tlaxcala they regrouped and, under Cortés's inspiring leadership, returned to lay siege to Tenochtitlán. They cut off the food supply and knocked down the aqueduct bringing fresh water. They also bombarded the buildings, shoveling the ruins into the lake as they advanced. Their best weapon proved to be smallpox, a disease brought from Europe, which killed the defenders in thousands. At last, twelve years after Cortés had landed at Veracruz, the Aztecs were forced to surrender. Their marvelous city was razed to the ground, and their gold and silver treasures shipped off to Spain.

Left: When it came to battle, the Spanish soldiers were far outnumbered, but their greatest "weapon" was their belief that their cause was blessed by God.

The Inca Empire

Rumors of golden cities brought Spaniards flocking to the New World. One band of tough, ambitious men, led by Vasco Nuñez de Balboa, came from Santo Domingo (now the Dominican Republic) to Central America. They traveled across the narrow isthmus of Darien (Panama), and became the first Europeans to set eyes on the Pacific Ocean.

Among Balboa's band was a former pig-keeper named Francisco Pizarro, who settled down in Darien. He searched for gold, explored the coast, and listened to stories of a great kingdom in the south. When he had collected enough evidence, he went to Spain to ask permission to conquer this unknown kingdom on behalf of the king. Permission was given; Pizarro returned to Darien and, in 1531, set out on his expedition of conquest. He had about 180 men and 27 horses.

The empire of the Incas stretched for half the length of South America. The Incas were a mountain people whose capital city, Cuzco, lay in the Andes of Peru more than 9,000 feet above sea level. Like the Aztecs, the Incas were a conquering race who ruled over many subject nations. Their hereditary ruler, the Inca, was believed to be descended from the god of the sun.

Pizarro's little band sailed down the coast from Darien. When they landed on the Peruvian coast, the Inca empire was involved in civil war. From his base at Quito (now in Ecuador), Atahualpa had just overthrown his half-brother to make himself Inca. That was a stroke of luck for the Spaniards. They went to meet Atahualpa at Cajamarca, exchanging polite messages as they approached and receiving a friendly welcome from the people they met on the way. Pizarro requested a meeting with Atahualpa. The next day the Inca entered the great square of Cajamarca with about 3,000 attendants. Meanwhile, Pizarro had stationed his men in the surrounding buildings.

The interview between the ruler of

Above: Machu Picchu, the most famous and best-preserved of Inca cities, was a great mountain fortress more than 1,500 feet above one of the gorges running through the Andes.

Below: When Atahualpa threw down the Bible, the Spaniards attacked his men with guns and cannon. Many were killed and Atahualpa was captured, later to be strangled by the Spanish.

Above and right: The Incas made beautiful objects of gold, such as this ceremonial knife, vase in the form of an animal-god, and plate showing the seed time for different crops.

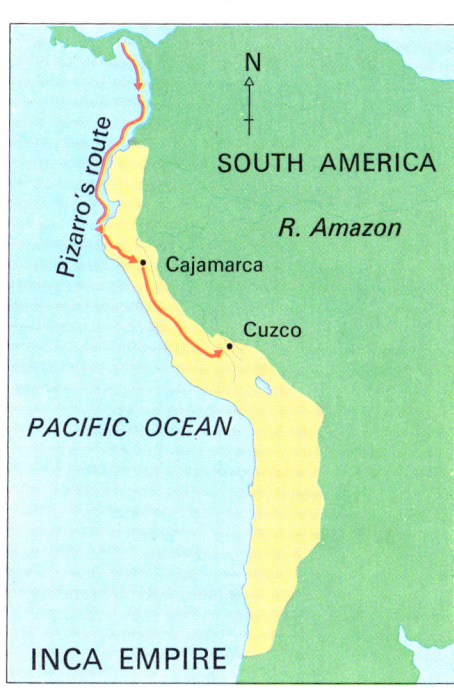

a great empire and the captain of a band of soldiers, carried on through an interpreter, was extraordinary. Pizarro delivered a short lecture on Christianity and demanded that the Inca should declare himself a Christian and a subject of the king of Spain. Not surprisingly he refused, and flung the Bible he had been given on the floor. The Spaniards immediately attacked and the Inca's men, who had few or no weapons, were routed. Pizarro himself grabbed the Inca and, while protecting him from attack, received a wound. Cuzco fell to the Spaniards, and the Inca empire was over, destroyed by a few hundred men.

The gold and silver captured in Cuzco made a rich man of every Spaniard there. But fate was to avenge the Incas, for the victors soon fell to quarreling among themselves. Within a few years, most of them were dead, many (like Pizarro himself) murdered by their own comrades.

Pizarro's men found that movement through the dense forests and steep mountains was hard and dangerous. Nevertheless, they carried out many long journeys of exploration. In 1539 a group led by one of Francisco Pizarro's brothers, Gonzalo, set out to gain land for themselves in the east. They left Quito on Christmas Day and, accompanied by hundreds of Indians, struggled over the mountains in heavy snow. On the other side they found themselves in a wet and empty region. Gonzalo Pizarro sent Francisco de Orellana down one of the rivers to look for food. The current took Orellana's canoe down to a great river, which he named the Amazon. He drifted downstream, and reached the sea, the first man to cross the continent of South America.

Gonzalo Pizarro staggered back to Quito. He had started with 1,000 men. He returned with less than 100.

Left: By the end of the 15th century, the Inca armies, from their base in the Cuzco valley, had conquered an area extending from Ecuador, in the north, to Chile.

The Discovery of North America

Columbus was not the only man to think of reaching the east by sailing to the west. John Cabot, who was born in Genoa (like Columbus) in 1450, came to England with his family when he was about 30 years old. In 1497, five years after Columbus's voyage, he set out from Bristol in search of a passage to Asia. He sailed with the blessing of King Henry VII and the backing of the Bristol merchants, who hoped they would soon be importing spices from the lands that Cabot would discover.

Cabot had a single ship, the *Matthew*, with a crew of eighteen. Less than 70 feet long, she was tossed about on the broad Atlantic like a cork in a stream. But she was sturdy and well-built, and sailed well before the wind. Cabot knew that Columbus had discovered islands in the west. He meant to be the first to reach the mainland, and his more northerly route would keep him well

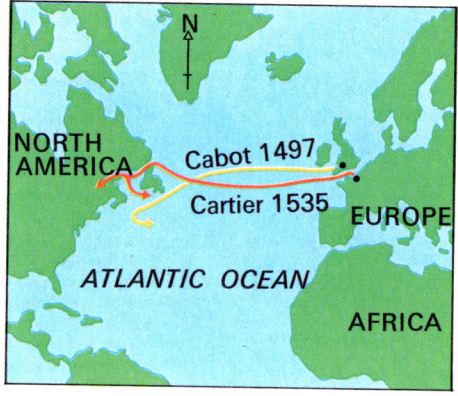

Above: Routes taken by Cabot and Cartier to North America.

Right: Cartier's arrival in Canada: a detail from a world map (here shown upside-down) made after his first voyage.

Below: Indian tribes along the St Lawrence River lived by fishing and hunting moose. Their canoes were made of bark.

away from the Spanish discoveries. Though his distance across the Atlantic was slightly shorter, Cabot's voyage took longer because the winds were less favorable.

On June 24, after 52 days at sea, land was sighted—a long, quiet coast lined with pine trees. The *Matthew* anchored in a bay. Cabot stepped ashore to claim this 'New Found Land', as he called it, in the name of the king of England. He was convinced that he was on the eastern shore of the Asian mainland. He cruised down the coast a few miles and returned to England to report.

Next year he sailed again. This time he had five ships, loaded with trade goods to exchange for Chinese silks and perfume. But he found no

Below: Indian tribes along the St Lawrence River lived by fishing and hunting moose. Their canoes were made of bark.

Chinese, only Indians dressed in skins. It became obvious that he had not found Asia at all and he turned back, a disappointed man.

Though the English followed Cabot's route in order to catch cod off Newfoundland, they lost interest in the New World and made no more discoveries for eighty years. Meanwhile the French, encouraged by King Francis I, made their appearance in North America.

By 1534, when Jacques Cartier sailed there with two ships, the route to Newfoundland was well-known. Although it was early May when he arrived, he had to wait a few days for ice to melt before sailing farther north. He explored the coast of Labrador, which he said was so grim and barren that it might have been the land that God gave to Cain. He sailed southward through the Strait of Belle Isle and was blown by a storm into the Gulf of St Lawrence. He found the mouth of a great river (the St Lawrence) which he hoped would be a sea passage through the New World to Asia. But, as winter was approaching, he decided to postpone his exploration until the next year.

In 1535 he sailed up the St Lawrence to the place where Quebec is now. He made his headquarters there for the winter and, guided by the Indians, took rowing boats to explore the river farther upstream. He got as far as Hochelega, an Indian town and the future site of Montreal.

As a rule, Cartier was on good terms with the Huron and Iroquois Indians, though he was shocked by their poverty. He said that there were no poorer people in the whole world. The Indians thought he came from heaven. They brought their sick for him to heal, while he read the Bible to them sitting under an oak tree. They told him stories of a mysterious kingdom, rich in jewels, up the Ottawa River. He never found this kingdom or a sea passage to Asia. But his journeys took him nearly 1,000 miles from the sea, and he explored more of North America than anyone else until the next century.

Around the World in 1082 Days

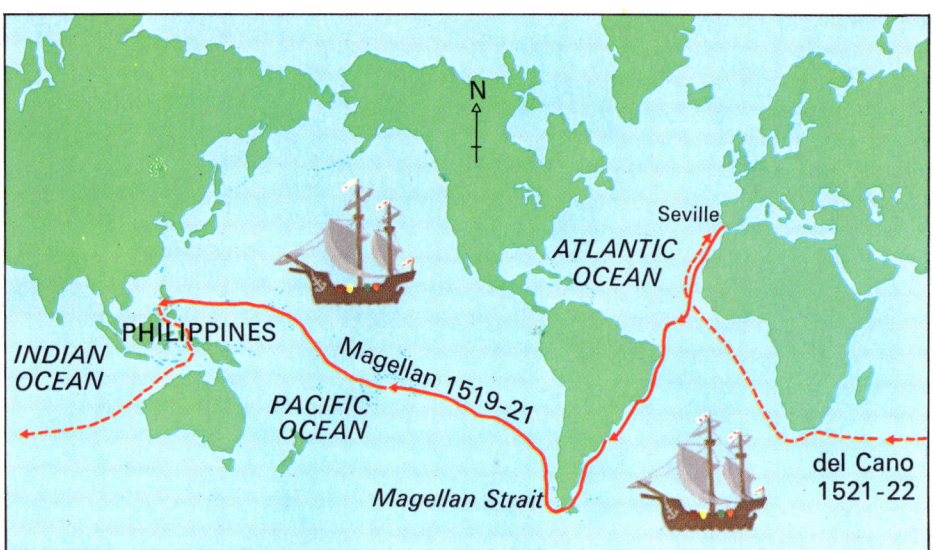

Above: Magellan searched for a strait in the far south of South America through to the Far East. It was a very difficult passage. Later, ships found a slightly easier way, farther south around Cape Horn.

The discovery of a New World on the other side of the Atlantic was a disappointment to those who had hoped to sail direct to Asia. Although the New World contained riches, too, it was an obstacle in the way of the route to the East. That was the object of Magellan's voyage. The Portuguese had already found a south-eastern route, via the Cape of Good Hope. The Spaniards, led by a Portuguese, Ferdinand Magellan, set out to find a route to Asia via the south-west.

In 1494 the Spaniards and the Portuguese had agreed that the undiscovered world should be divided in two. The dividing line was drawn through the middle of the Atlantic. West of the line was the Spanish half, including all the Americas except Brazil, which projected over the line into the Portuguese half. The eastern or Portuguese half included Africa and India. On the other, unknown, side of the world, it was uncertain just where the dividing line ran. Magellan and his supporters realized that if they sailed far enough to the west they would come into the Portuguese half. But they believed that at least some of the Spice Islands were within the Spanish half. Those islands were Magellan's destination.

Magellan's plan was approved by the king of Spain in 1517, and in August 1519 he set sail. He had 260

men and five ships. Although only one ship, the *Victoria*, was to return safely, they were well-made merchant vessels, and looked similar to Columbus's ship.

Like Columbus, Magellan was a foreigner in charge of a Spanish expedition, and he also had trouble with his men. Some of the officers did not like him either. That was partly his own fault as he was a prickly character who refused to inform them of his plans.

Matters came to a crisis in cold, grim Patagonia in South America, where the first winter was spent after the long voyage through the Atlantic. Fortunately for Magellan, he was warned that a mutiny was planned. He kept his control by using severe measures. The chief Spanish officer was marooned on that unfriendly shore, and was never seen again. Several men were executed as a warning to the others.

Magellan was confident that he would find a strait in South America which would lead him to the Pacific. Although the entrance is difficult to see even for a captain who knows it is

Above: Magellan's ships battle through the Strait.

Left and above left: In Patagonia the explorers saw animals they had never seen before: penguins and guanacos (a type of llama).

there, Magellan found his strait (now named after him). He led his ships, now reduced to three, through it. The passage was difficult. Ice-topped mountains loomed on either side, and the wind blew like fury dead against the ships. It took 38 days to pass through, though later captains took much longer.

Magellan had no idea of the immense size of the ocean that lay before him. He expected to cross it in a week or two. In fact he was at sea without sighting land for nearly four months. Conditions on the *Victoria* were desperate. The drinking water turned yellow and stinking, and the last of the ship's biscuit was eaten. The starving sailors stripped the leather off the *yards* (spars supporting the sails), soaked it in sea water and toasted it—then ate it. They ate

sawdust from the planks and chased rats—a luxury—in the hold. Many died of scurvy before the ships reached Guam, where at last they got fresh supplies of food and water.

They called at the Ladrones or Thieves' Islands, so named because the local people took everything they could lay their hands on. Then they sailed on to the Philippines. Magellan foolishly became involved in a local tribal war there and was killed during a battle.

Under a new captain, Sebastian del Cano, the *Victoria* reached the Moluccas—the Spice Islands— toward the end of 1521. The Spaniards took on a cargo of cloves and burned one ship, as there were not enough men left to sail her. The captain of the other ship chose to go home the way they had come, but never made it. Meanwhile del Cano took the *Victoria* on across the Indian Ocean, around the Cape of Good Hope, and home through the Atlantic. He reached Seville in September 1522. Only eighteen men, looking more like skeletons, remained alive to tell how they had sailed around the world.

The North-West Passage

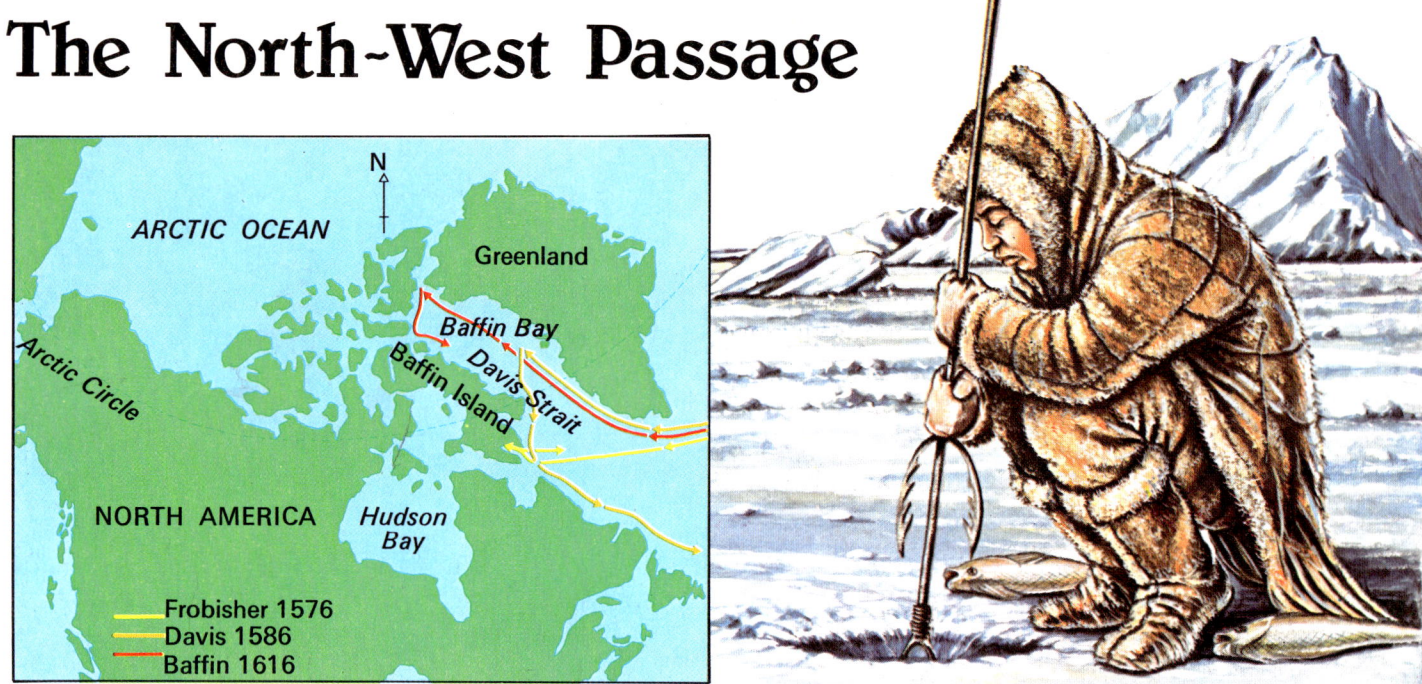

ARCTIC OCEAN

Greenland

Baffin Bay

Davis Strait

Baffin Island

Arctic Circle

NORTH AMERICA

Hudson Bay

Frobisher 1576
Davis 1586
Baffin 1616

The search for a sea route to the Spice Islands and the Far East had been one of the main reasons for the early European voyages of discovery. This search did not stop when the Americas and the Pacific Ocean were discovered. The Portuguese had discovered a south-east route. The Spaniards, thanks to Magellan, had found a south-west route, though it was so long that few ships used it. The northern countries of Europe searched for a sea passage in the north-east or north-west.

In the north-west, England took the lead. Nothing much came of John Cabot's pioneering voyages in 1497-98 until Martin Frobisher renewed the search in 1576. He sailed in May down the river Thames, passing the palace at Greenwich where Queen Elizabeth stood in the window waving her handkerchief.

After a very cold and stormy crossing, land was sighted and Frobisher sailed into the deep bay in northern Canada now bearing his name. The Inuit or Eskimos there looked like Asians to English eyes, and Frobisher thought he must be sailing along a strait that divided Asia from America.

Next year he sailed again to explore his "strait" more thoroughly. He made a poor job of it. From his first voyage he had brought back some mineral ore which glittered yellow. Those who saw it believed Frobisher had found

Above left: The map shows the routes taken by Frobisher, Davis and Baffin in the struggle to find the North-West Passage. There is more than one sea route through Arctic Canada, but parts of these are often heavily choked with

gold. On his second expedition he was less interested in the North-West Passage than in loading his ships with ore which, in the end, turned out to be completely worthless.

Frobisher's work was continued in the 1580s by John Davis who was interested in every person or thing he saw, not just in getting rich. Frobisher had fired guns at the Eskimos. Davis preferred to play football with them.

Davis sailed around south Greenland, which he called the "Land of Desolation". He then went northward through Davis Strait (named after him) as far as the Arctic Circle. He crossed the strait, dodging the pack ice, and explored the bays and inlets of northern Canada, hoping to find the North-West Passage.

One of the inlets that Davis did not investigate was Hudson's Strait. A strong tide runs out of the strait, which probably discouraged Davis from entering. That task was left to the explorer Henry Hudson, after whom the strait is named.

When Hudson, in the *Discovery*, reached Hudson's Strait in 1610, he sailed boldly through, against 'a great

ice, even in the summer. They are too difficult to be of use as regular shipping lanes.

Above: Eskimos hunted fish and seals through holes cut in the ice when the sea was frozen.

and whirling sea', and found himself in Hudson Bay. He thought he must have found the North-West Passage, and that the coasts of Asia must lie on the other side of the 'sea' he had discovered. As he explored the waters of the bay in wintry fog and ice, his men began to grumble, as seamen always did when far from home. They soon had good cause for complaint for Hudson had left his departure too late. The way home was blocked by ice. He and his men were forced to spend a miserable winter in Hudson Bay, wondering how long the food would last.

The *Discovery* was unable to move until the following summer, but everyone knew there was not enough food for the voyage home. Led by Robert Juet, who had served as mate under Hudson on an earlier voyage, the crew rebelled. They put Hudson, his young son and five loyal sailors into a boat, and set them adrift without food or weapons. It was little better than murder: no trace of them was ever found. As for the mutineers, four were killed soon afterwards in a fight with Eskimos. Robert Juet died

Above: A modern ice-breaker can force a way through the kind of thick ice that defeated the early explorers in the Arctic.

Right: Hudson, his son and a few loyal sailors, were left to die.

of starvation on the voyage home. Only a few lived to see England again. The brilliant English navigator William Baffin used the *Discovery* in his attempt to find the North-West Passage in 1616. Baffin sailed up Davis Strait but continued up to the northern end of the bay named after him. Unfortunately, Lancaster Sound, which leads through to the North-West Passage, was blocked with ice. Baffin thought there was no way through, and sailed for home.

Although many later captains tried to find a North-West Passage in Arctic Canada, no one succeeded in navigating it by ship until nearly 300 years after Hudson. The Norwegian, Roald Amundsen, forced a way through from the Atlantic to the Pacific, but it took three years, and few ships have managed it since.

China and Japan

In the 13th century, before the Age of Discovery began, the Far East was not completely cut off from Europe. Merchants from Italy occasionally traveled as far as China. The most famous of them was a Venetian named Marco Polo, who entered the service of Kublai Khan, the Tartar emperor of China. Marco Polo remained in the Far East for more than 20 years, visiting Burma, India and Indonesia.

In many ways civilization in the East was far ahead of Europe. In China Marco Polo saw many things familiar to us but strange to him, such as asbestos cloth, coal-burning fires, dishes of porcelain, paper money and

Above: Marco Polo embarks at Venice for his journey to China.

river bridges 1000 feet long. A great city like Hangchow, with its pavilions, canals and broad carriageways, made Venice look like "a dirty village" according to Marco. His description of China was generally truthful, although he often exaggerated. He reported some very tall stories, like the one about the great bird of Madagascar which seized elephants in its talons and dropped them from a great height. His book, which is called *Travels of Marco Polo*, was popular, but it was treated as a typical

Above: The civilization of China was much older, and in many ways far in advance of, society in medieval Europe.

Above: Father Matteo Ricci.

Below: The Polos travel across Asia in an embassy caravan.

traveler's tale, more fiction than fact.

After Marco Polo, there were few contacts between Europe and China until the Portuguese arrived in the south in the early 16th century. The Ming dynasty, which ruled from Peking, discouraged contact with foreigners, including the Portuguese.

As in other parts of the world, some of the earliest European travelers in the Far East were Roman Catholic missionaries belonging to the order known as the *Jesuits*. A Jesuit from Navarre, named Francis Xavier, was the first man to give an accurate account of Japan. He was delighted with the Japanese, admiring their sense of honor, their courtesy and their moderate way of life. There seemed to him to be little active religion in Japan and therefore, he supposed, the Japanese would be ideal converts to Christianity. But here he ran into a problem. The Japanese were admirers of the great learning and culture of China. They were surprised to find that Jesus Christ was entirely unknown to the wise men of China. Francis Xavier realized that, if he hoped to convert the Japanese, he would have to convert the Chinese first. He set out for China but died before he reached it, in 1552.

In the same year Matteo Ricci was born in Italy. When he grew up he entered the Jesuit order and was sent to Goa, in Portuguese India. There he learned Chinese, and in 1583 gained permission to settle in Canton.

In this way Francis Xavier's dream that Christianity should be preached in China came true.

Father Ricci was a remarkable man and, in many ways, far ahead of his time. He recognized that Chinese civilization was as old and diverse as anything in Europe, and that it would be absurd to try to force Christianity down Chinese throats. The methods that might work among simple people would not work there. So he became a kind of Chinese wise man himself. He dressed in the Chinese way, and built his church in the Chinese style. He won friends by his knowledge of science and geography, and in his teaching he concentrated on the ethical ideals of Christianity rather than its religious doctrines. He even allowed his converts to continue some non-Christian forms of religion, such as ancestor-worship.

Father Ricci's great ambition was to get to Peking, for he knew he could do little without the support of the emperor. In 1600 permission was at last granted: he entered the 'forbidden city' and was well received by the emperor, Wan-Li. He had brought presents, among them a clock which especially delighted the emperor.

Wan-Li agreed to hang a picture of Jesus in the imperial apartments, and from that time Christianity was tolerated in China. The Jesuits made many advances in geographical knowledge, as well as making religious converts.

Cook's Pacific

On his voyage to the Pacific which lasted from 1768 and 1771, the English explorer Lieutenant James Cook had not proved that a southern continent did not exist. In 1772 he sailed on a second voyage in search of it. His plan was simple. He would simply sail to a far southern latitude and then circle the world. If the continent was there, he would be bound to strike it.

This time he took two ships, the *Resolution* and the *Adventure*. Like his first ship, the *Endeavour*, they were both *colliers* (in fact all

Right: This map of the Pacific shows Captain Cook's last voyage.

Below and below right: Breadfruit was the staple diet of South Pacific Islanders. The artist in the *Endeavour*, Sydney Parkinson, painted this plant and also sketched the kangeroo.

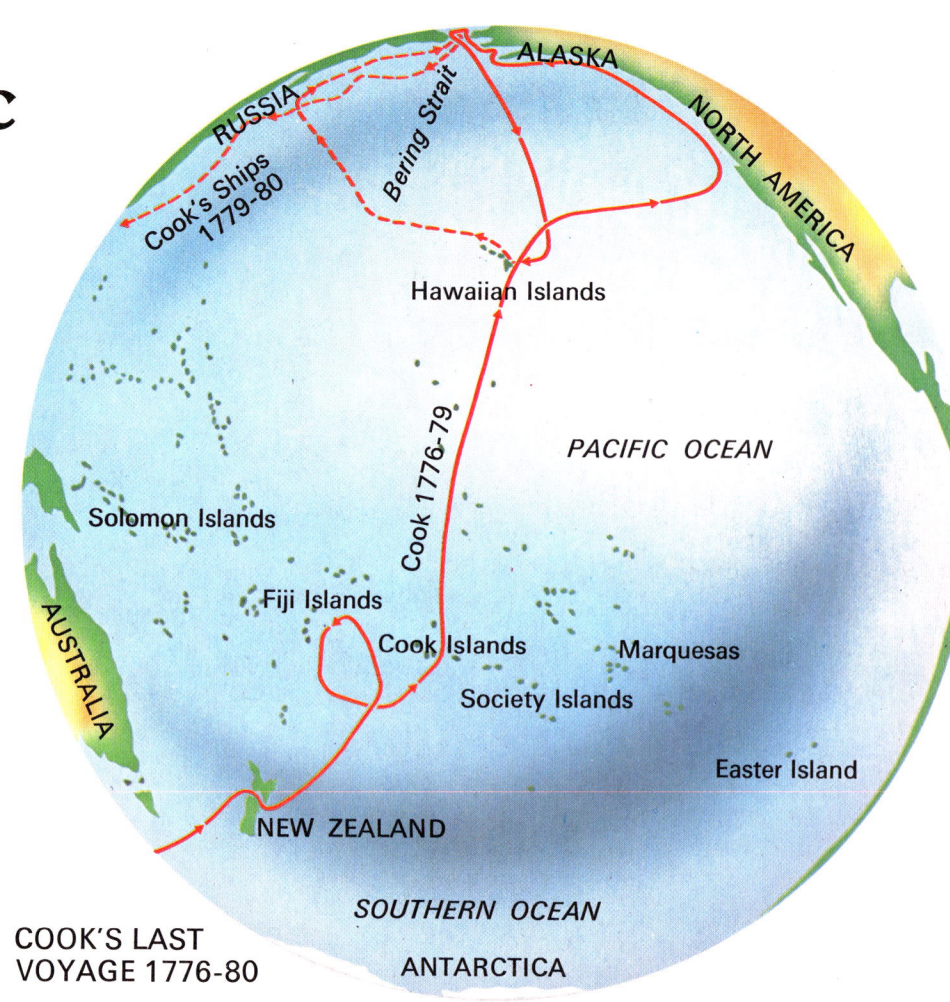

COOK'S LAST VOYAGE 1776-80

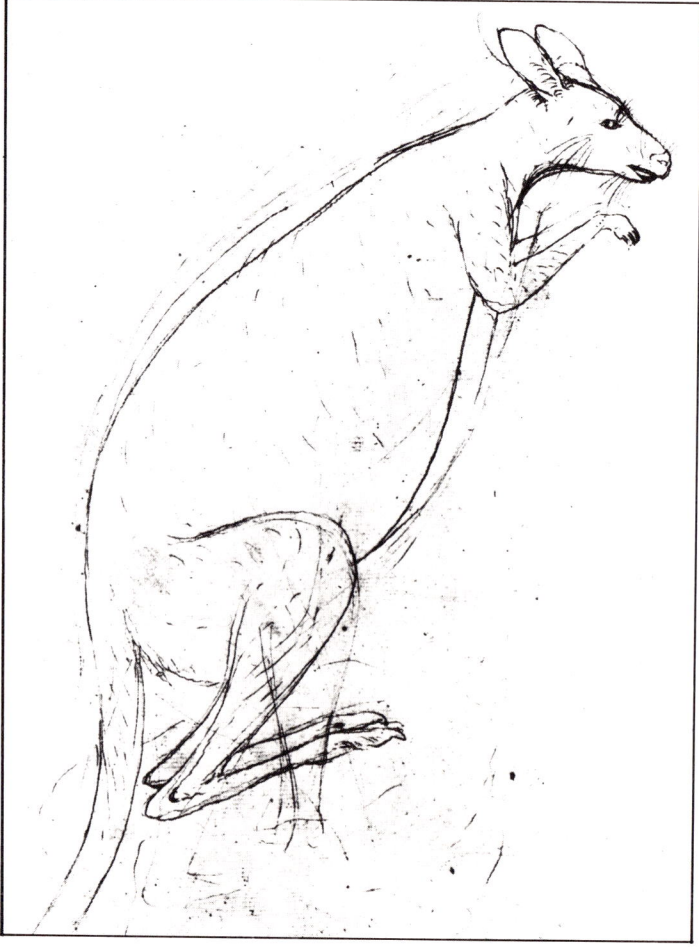

three were built in the same Whitby shipyard). The botanist, Joseph Banks, who had accompanied Cook before, wanted to go again, but he insisted on a larger ship and more artists and scientists. His demands were refused so he went off to Iceland instead, and another scientist, J. R. Forster, was appointed. Forster was a less agreeable character than Banks, but he did sacrifice his pet dog to make a tasty soup for Cook when he was ill in the Southern Ocean.

At the beginning of 1773 the ships reached the Antarctic Circle south of the Cape of Good Hope. The sails stiffened and the ropes froze as hard as iron bars. Huge flat icebergs drifted past on a gray sea. Ordering extra nips of spirits for all hands, Cook sailed east. The ships became separated, but met again in New Zealand where they spent the winter. The following year they sailed south and east again, crossing the Antarctic Circle at two points but each time forced northward by ice. The third summer Cook passed Cape Horn and completed the third and final section of his circle around the world when he crossed his own route south of the Cape of Good Hope.

The *Resolution* had been farther south than any ship before. New islands had been discovered, but no mainland. Although he came near at several points, Cook never sighted the true southern continent, Antarctica. But the voyage had proved that, if a southern continent

Above: During Cook's last voyage, in search of the North-West Passage, his men organized hunting parties to shoot walrus.

Below: The death of Cook in Hawaii due, it seems, to a misunderstanding, was a tragic end to a great career.

did exist, it could hardly be any larger than Antarctica actually is.

Cook's third voyage had a different purpose: to seek the North-West Passage. Unlike earlier searchers, he began by seeking the Pacific exit of the passage. He sailed, again in the *Resolution*, via South Africa and New Zealand, and called at some of his favorite stopping places in the Pacific on his way north.

Cruising north with the trade winds, the *Resolution* sailed up the coast of Alaska and entered the Bering Strait. Cook continued north until forced back by the drifting Arctic ice. In the strait, Cook's men had the exciting experience, denied to Bering when he had entered these waters, of seeing Asia on one side and North America on the other.

In November 1778 Cook made his most important discovery when he came upon the island group known as Hawaii. The Hawaiians spoke, like the Maoris, a version of the same language as the people of Tahiti. Cook was amazed by this evidence of how the Polynesian people had spread themselves over the vast Pacific Ocean at some time in the past. The Europeans were not the only ocean-going race.

The Hawaiians, like the Tahitians, were friendly. Simpler people than the Tahitians, they thought that Cook's men were supernatural creatures, and sang hymns in their honor. This time Cook would let no women on his ships, hoping to prevent the spread of venereal disease which European sailors had inflicted on other Pacific islanders. But trade was brisk—iron nails were exchanged for fresh pork.

Unfortunately, good relations did not last. Quarrels broke out over the theft of one of the ship's boats, guns were fired and a Hawaiian chief killed. Cook, standing at the water's edge, turned to signal to the boats, and was stabbed fatally in the back. Sadly, the ships made their way home, bringing the remains of the greatest of all maritime explorers to their last resting place in Westminster Abbey.

The Discovery of the World

In the three centuries that passed between the time the Portuguese set out on the first cautious exploration of the Atlantic and the last voyage of Captain Cook, Europe discovered the world. In the 15th century Europeans knew only their own continent, part of Asia, and the northern fringes of Africa. More than half the world was a total blank, and much of the rest was known only in dim outline. No European ships had sailed in any of the great oceans except the eastern edges of the Atlantic. The existence of the Pacific, an ocean so large that if all the continents were dropped into it they would sink without trace, was unsuspected.

The discovery of the world was, more exactly, the discovery of the oceans. All the oceans and the seas are connected, so it is possible to sail from any port in the world to any other sea coast. That is what Europeans learned to do. From Columbus to Cook, they sought out all the world's waterways and charted, not always accurately, all the shores that enclosed them. A map of the world after Cook showed the seas and continents much as we know them today, with nearly every island, as well as larger lands, in place. There was only one omission—Antarctica. Its existence was suspected (the icebergs of the south were a likely sign of land somewhere), and in better weather Cook might have sighted it.

Yet in one sense the discovery of the world had only just begun. The position and shape of the islands and continents was known, but not what lay beyond their coasts. The Portuguese sailed around Africa before the end of the 15th century, but at the time of Cook's death Europeans had hardly traveled beyond Africa's coastal plains. No one had penetrated the interior of Australia or New Zealand. Prosperous colonies existed in the Americas, yet the country which was soon to declare its independence as the United States of America was mostly unexplored west of the Mississippi River. Northern and western Canada was unknown territory. Huge areas of South America had never seen a European face, not even the serious, inquiring face of a Jesuit missionary. To explore the newly-discovered lands was the task of the 19th century. Even today there are some places, for example, parts of the Amazon Basin in Brazil, which have never been thoroughly mapped.

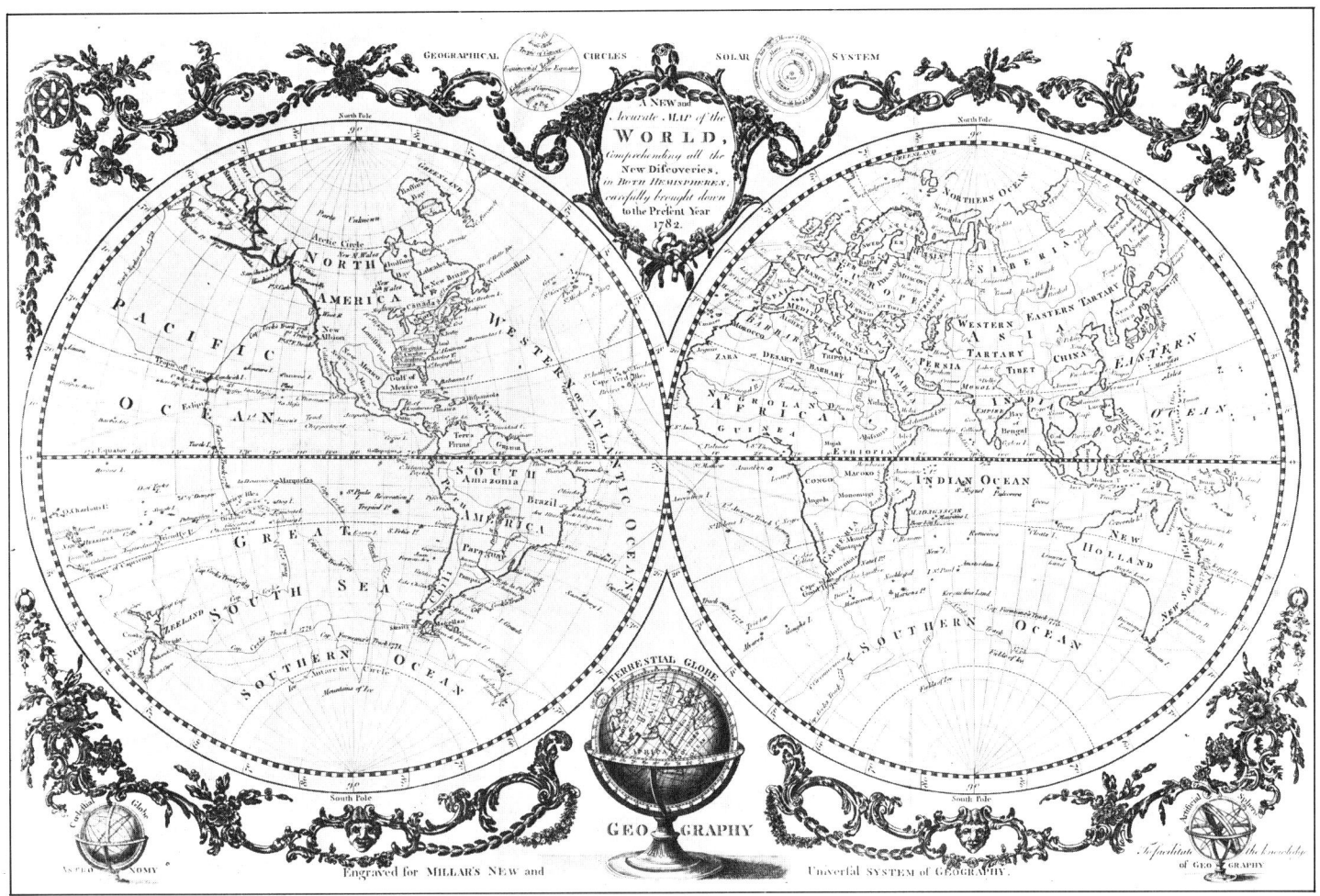

Left: This map shows the world as it was known to educated

Europeans in 1486 on the eve of the age of discovery. It was based

on descriptions of the world by the Greek geographer Ptolemy who lived in Alexandria in the second century A.D. It is a great improvement on the medieval map on page 2.

In the 300 years before Cook, the precision of maps, charts, instruments, and methods of navigation had improved enormously. Columbus would have been as bewildered by Cook's instruments as Cook would be by the instruments in an airplane pilot's cockpit. When Columbus was in the West Indies he had believed he was on the other side of the world. Cook's calculation of the position of New Zealand was correct to within a mile or so. On his second voyage Cook carried a *chronometer* of the type invented a few years earlier by a Yorkshire clockmaker, John Harrison. This was perhaps the single most important advance in navigational methods. The chronometer at last allowed even a navigator less expert than Cook to measure longitude exactly and

without great difficulty. This overcame a problem which had troubled every long-distance voyager since Columbus.

Although the chronometer, and a host of other aids, had made navigation less of a gamble, basic methods had not changed so much. Cook's ship was larger and more reliable, though not much faster, than the early caravels or the ships of Magellan. It was still a wooden vessel, relying wholly on the winds to drive it. The story of the discovery of the world is the story of the triumph of the sailing ship.

Discovery often led to colonization and conquest. It happened with Cortés in Mexico and Pizarro in Peru, and it happened in other countries too. Eventually, most of Africa and much of Asia, as well as North and South

Above: Ptolemy's map was still a far cry from this world map which includes Captain Cook's discoveries. The only major outline that remains to be added is that of Antarctica.

America, came under the control of Europeans. That was not the purpose of the discoverers, who were usually seeking trade rather than conquest. All the same, the discoveries of Columbus, Pizarro and their successors did lead finally to the dominance of Europeans. This had, and still has, a tremendous influence on the way people throughout the world think and feel and live.

Lifelines

Christopher Columbus (1451-1506) →

On his first voyage in 1492, this Italian navigator discovered Cuba and Haiti as well as smaller West Indian islands. Columbus then returned in triumph to Spain. He was sent out again the next year with 17 ships to establish colonies in the newly-discovered lands. The expedition was a disappointment. The men left in Haiti the previous year had all died, and Columbus was unable to find Zipangu and Cathay (Japan and China) which he was convinced lay nearby. The first colonial town was built at Santo Domingo. Columbus then discovered Jamaica. On his third voyage (1498) he discovered the Orinoco River in South America, which he believed flowed from Paradise. At Santo Domingo quarrels broke out and for a time Columbus was thrown in chains by the Spanish governor. He kept the chains, a bitter reminder of his humiliation, for the rest of his life. His fourth and last voyage (1502) was also troubled by quarrels among the Spanish settlers, and by storms. He searched for a strait in Central America, and heard stories of a rich kingdom (probably the Inca empire) which he believed must be China. Columbus returned to Spain disappointed, and still unwilling to believe that he had discovered a continent unconnected with Asia or the Spice Islands.

James Cook (1728-79)

A Yorkshireman of Scots descent, he learned the ways of the sea in Whitby colliers, the same type of ship in which he made his exploring voyages. At the age of 27 he joined the Royal Navy as an able seaman. Intelligent and methodical, he was far above the usual standard of British seaman and soon rose to be master of a ship (below the captain). During the Seven Years' War he took part in the siege of Quebec (1759) and learnt how to make charts and surveys. After the war he gained a high reputation for his charts of Newfoundland waters, which he published at his own expense. In spite of the influence of several high-ranking officers who had gained a good opinion of him as former commanders, he was a surprising choice as captain of the *Endeavour* in 1768 because he was not a 'gentleman'. He only obtained an officer rank in 1768, and did not become a captain until after his second voyage. Cook was not a very colourful character, but was a brilliant navigator whose skill was admired by sailors all over the world. Even the French government, then at war with England, allowed his ship free passage. In spite (or because) of his humble background and lack of education, he showed rare intelligence and compassion in his dealings with rough seamen or Pacific islanders.

Hernán Cortés (1485-1547)

Cortés was an adventurous, hard-drinking Spanish soldier, but also an intelligent and ambitious man. He hoped to create a vast territory for himself in Mexico. As well as conquering the Aztecs, he had to fight jealous Spaniards, and returned to Spain to get the support of the king, Charles V. When he returned to Mexico with his position confirmed, he concentrated on building up his power. But the appointment of a new Spanish viceroy of Mexico led to more quarrels and another trip home for some royal support. Even though Cortés had served with the Spanish forces in the siege of Algiers (1541), for which he had to borrow a suit of armour from the Spanish secretary of state, he was coldly received this time by the king. 'Who is this presumptuous man?' the king asked. To which Cortés replied, 'I am the man who has given you more kingdoms than your ancestors left you towns'. He died in Spain, almost forgotten, a few years later.

Ferdinand Magellan
(1480-1521)

As a young man this Portuguese captain fought for his country in the Far East, taking part in the siege of Malacca (1511) and sailing in search of spice islands. In 1514 he was fighting in Morocco, where he received a wound that left him with a permanent limp. Back in Portugal, Magellan was slighted by the king. He felt his honour had been insulted, and entered the service of Charles V, king of Spain, who gave him command of the voyage to the Pacific via South America (1519). Magellan had probably been thinking over a plan to reach the Spice Islands from the west for many years. In the Philippines he made an alliance with the king of Cebu and was killed by the king's enemies in Mactan.

Francisco Pizarro
(1475-1541)

A Spanish adventurer from a poor family, Pizarro was as tough and brutal as Cortés but less intelligent. He sailed to America in 1509. After his remarkable conquest of the Incas, he organized the running of silver mines in Peru and built a new capital at Lima, on the coast. Pizarro ruled the north of the Inca kingdom and Diego de Almagro, one of his companions on the first expedition from Panama, ruled the south. Each tried to increase his territory at the expense of the other, but in 1538 Pizarro captured Almagro and had

him killed. Three years later, a group of Almagro's men murdered Pizarro in the palace he had built for himself.

Marco Polo
(1254-1324)

Marco Polo, here on his travels, was a boy in Venice when his father and uncle returned from a journey to China. They decided to take him with them on a second expedition. They travelled overland, crossing the high

Pamir mountains and the Gobi desert. The Great Khan, Mongol ruler of China, took a fancy to the young Marco and made him his servant. Twenty years passed before the Polos returned, in 1296, by sea from China through the Indian Ocean to Ormuz, and from there to Constantinople (Istanbul). Marco's book about his travels made him famous. It also encouraged the belief that the Far East could be reached by crossing the Atlantic.